Pebble® Plus

President
Barack
Obama

by Jennifer L. Marks

Consulting Editor:
Gail Saunders-Smith, PhD

Consultant:
Andra Gillespie, PhD
Department of Political Science
Emory University, Atlanta, Georgia

Capstone press®

Mankato, Minnesota

Pebble Plus is published by Capstone Press,
151 Good Counsel Drive, P.O. Box 669, Mankato, Minnesota 56002.
www.capstonepress.com

Library of Congress Cataloging-in-Publication Data
Marks, Jennifer, 1979–
    President Barack Obama / by Jennifer L. Marks.
    p. cm.
    Includes bibliographical references and index.
    ISBN-13: 978-1-4296-3730-5 (hardcover)
    ISBN-13: 978-1-4296-3732-9 (softcover)
    1. Obama, Barack — Juvenile literature. 2. Presidents — United States — Biography — Juvenile literature.
I. Title.
E908.M37 2009
973.932092 — dc22 [B]   2009001081

Summary: Simple text and photographs describe the life of Barack Obama.

Editorial Credits

Erika L. Shores, editor; Veronica Bianchini, designer; Deirdre Barton, photo researcher

Photo Credits

AP Images, 11; Punahou Schools File, 13; Ron Lewis, 25; Seth Perlman, 17
Corbis/John Wrin/Harvard University, 15; Martin H. Simon, 19; Orjan F. Ellingvag/Dagbladet, 23; Reuters, 5, 7, 9
EMMANUEL DUNAND/AFP/Getty Images, cover
Getty Images/AFP/TIMOTHY A. CLARY, 27
Library of Congress, 29 (both)
Shutterstock/Alan Freed, 21; mistydawnphoto, 1
Wikipedia, public-domain image, 28 (both)

Note to Parents and Teachers

President Barack Obama supports national history standards related to people and culture. The
images support early readers in understanding the text. The repetition of words and phrases
helps early readers learn new words. This book also introduces early readers to subject-specific
vocabulary words, which are defined in the Glossary section. Early readers may need assistance
to read some words and to use the Table of Contents, Glossary, Read More, Internet Sites, and
Index sections of the book.

Table of Contents

Student of the World. 4

Adult Life 12

Making a Difference 16

Winning the Election 22

President Obama 26

Facts about Barack Obama . . . 28

Presidents of the United States. 29

Glossary 30

Read More 31

Internet Sites. 31

Index 32

Student of the World

Barack Obama was born
in Honolulu, Hawaii,
on August 4, 1961.
His mother, Ann Dunham,
was from a small town
in Kansas. His father, Barack
Obama Sr., was from Kenya.

born in Honolulu,
Hawaii

1961

Young Barack in Hawaii, date of photo unknown

Education was important
to Barack's parents.
When Barack was 2,
his father left to go to
Harvard University.
Barack stayed in Hawaii with
his mother and her parents.

born in Honolulu,
Hawaii

1961

Barack saw his father again in 1971.

In 1967, Barack and his mother

moved to Jakarta, Indonesia.

They lived with Lolo,

Ann's new husband.

Barack saw many poor people

in Jakarta. Their struggles

made him sad.

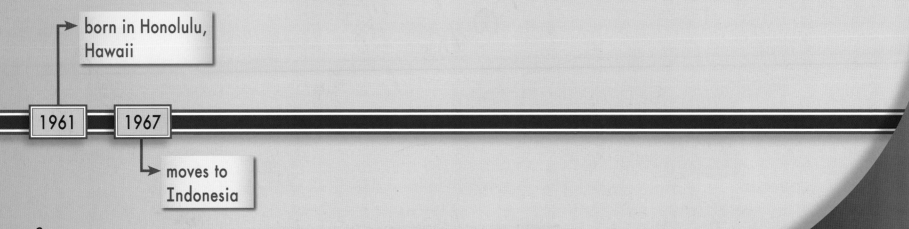

born in Honolulu,
Hawaii

1961   1967

moves to
Indonesia

Barack with his stepfather, his mother, and half sister Maya in 1968

Ann wanted the best for
her son. Barack could go to
a better school in Hawaii.
Barack returned there to live
with his grandparents.
He went to Punahou School
in Honolulu.

born in Honolulu,
Hawaii

1961   1967

moves to
Indonesia

Barack with his grandparents
at his high school graduation in 1979

Adult Life

Barack was a popular student
and a good basketball player.
After high school, he went
to college. He graduated from
Columbia University in 1983.
Then he moved to Chicago.
He worked to find people jobs.

born in Honolulu, Hawaii

graduates from Columbia University

1961   1967   1983

moves to Indonesia

Barack with his high school basketball team in 1977

In 1988, Barack left Chicago
to go to Harvard Law School.
He moved back to Chicago
when he finished.
In 1992, he married a lawyer
named Michelle Robinson.

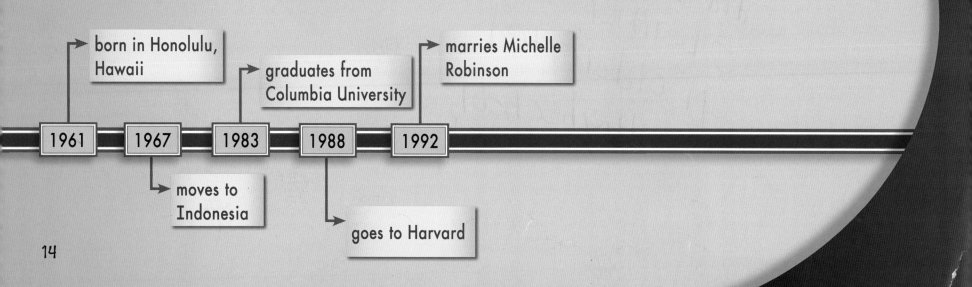

born in Honolulu,
Hawaii

graduates from
Columbia University

marries Michelle
Robinson

| 1961 | 1967 | 1983 | 1988 | 1992 |

moves to
Indonesia

goes to Harvard

Making a Difference

Barack was elected to the

Illinois state senate in 1996.

He wanted to improve

the state's schools.

He wanted equal rights

for all people.

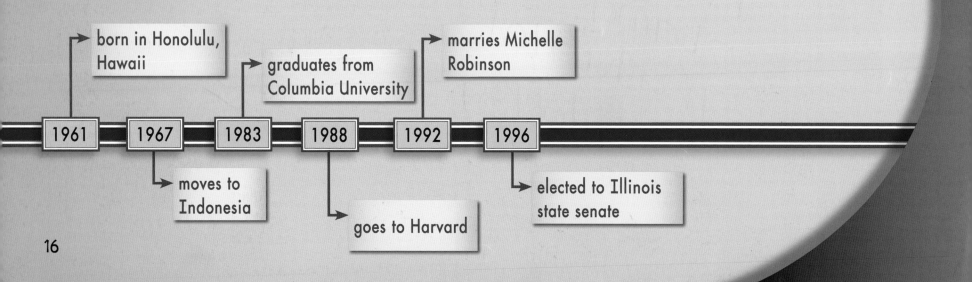

born in Honolulu,
Hawaii

graduates from
Columbia University

marries Michelle
Robinson

| 1961 | 1967 | 1983 | 1988 | 1992 | 1996 |

moves to
Indonesia

goes to Harvard

elected to Illinois
state senate

While he served in the Illinois senate, Barack's daughters Malia and Sasha were born. In 2004, Barack became a U.S. senator. He wanted to help make people's lives better. In 2007, he decided to run for president.

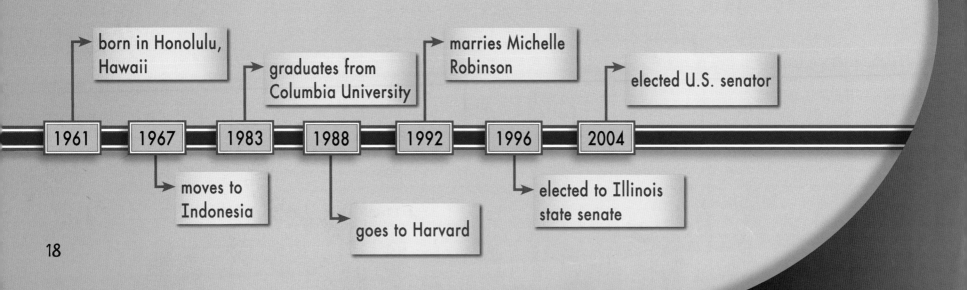

born in Honolulu, Hawaii

graduates from Columbia University

marries Michelle Robinson

elected U.S. senator

1961 | 1967 | 1983 | 1988 | 1992 | 1996 | 2004

moves to Indonesia

goes to Harvard

elected to Illinois state senate

Barack gave speeches
all over the country.
He spoke about jobs,
improving health care, and
ending the Iraq war. His words
gave people hope. Americans
voted on November 4, 2008.

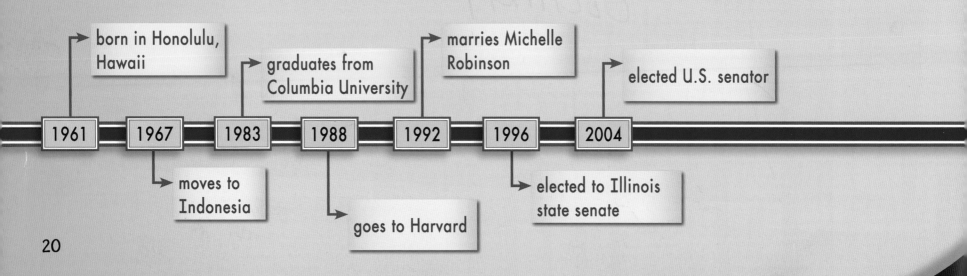

1961 — born in Honolulu, Hawaii

1967 — moves to Indonesia

1983 — graduates from Columbia University

1988 — goes to Harvard

1992 — marries Michelle Robinson

1996 — elected to Illinois state senate

2004 — elected U.S. senator

Winning the Election

By the end of the night,

Barack had won enough votes.

In Chicago, he gave

an acceptance speech.

The excited crowd cheered.

Many were moved to tears.

They shouted, "Yes, we can!"

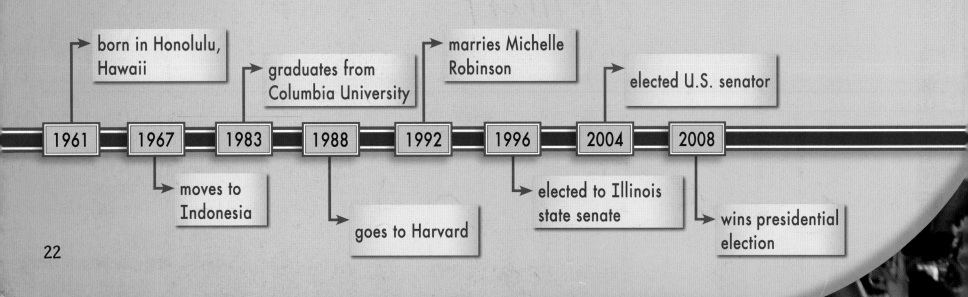

born in Honolulu, Hawaii

graduates from Columbia University

marries Michelle Robinson

elected U.S. senator

1961 1967 1983 1988 1992 1996 2004 2008

moves to Indonesia

goes to Harvard

elected to Illinois state senate

wins presidential election

The election made history. Barack was the first black president of the United States. Americans hoped Barack would bring even more changes to the country.

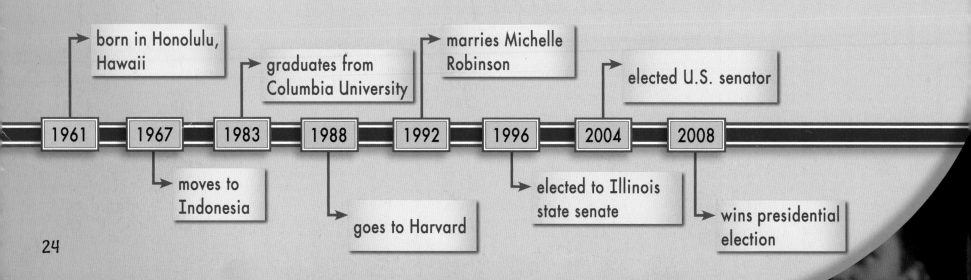

born in Honolulu, Hawaii

graduates from Columbia University

marries Michelle Robinson

elected U.S. senator

| 1961 | 1967 | 1983 | 1988 | 1992 | 1996 | 2004 | 2008 |

moves to Indonesia

goes to Harvard

elected to Illinois state senate

wins presidential election

President Obama

Barack Obama became
the 44th U.S. president
on January 20, 2009.
Leading the nation
wouldn't be easy.
President Obama was
ready for the challenge.

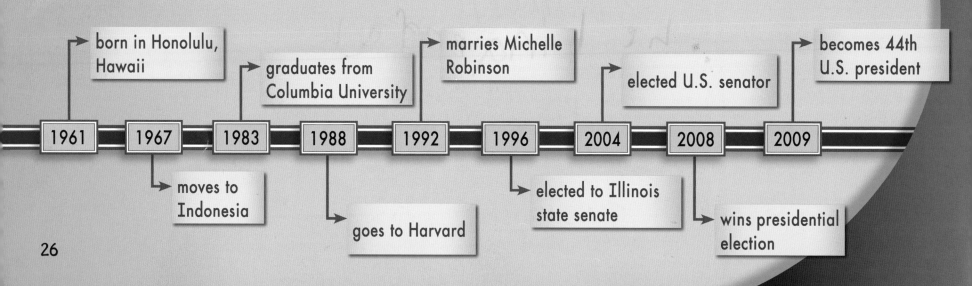

born in Honolulu,
Hawaii

graduates from
Columbia University

marries Michelle
Robinson

elected U.S. senator

becomes 44th
U.S. president

1961 1967 1983 1988 1992 1996 2004 2008 2009

moves to
Indonesia

goes to Harvard

elected to Illinois
state senate

wins presidential
election

Facts about Barack Obama

Born:
August 4, 1961

Parents:
Ann Dunham and Barack Obama Sr.

Wife:
Michelle Robinson Obama

Children:
Malia, born in 1998; Natasha, or Sasha
for short, born in 2001

Favorite book:
Song of Solomon by Toni Morrison

Favorite movies:
"Godfather I & II"

Favorite sport: basketball

Heroes:
Martin Luther King Jr., Mohandas Gandhi,
Pablo Picasso, and **John Coltrane**

Hobbies:
spending time with Malia and Sasha,
basketball, and writing

Presidents of the United States

George Washington, 1789–1797
John Adams, 1797–1801
Thomas Jefferson, 1801–1809
James Madison, 1809–1817
James Monroe, 1817–1825
John Quincy Adams, 1825–1829
Andrew Jackson, 1829–1837
Martin Van Buren, 1837–1841
William Henry Harrison, 1841
John Tyler, 1841–1845
James K. Polk, 1845–1849
Zachary Taylor, 1849–1850
Millard Fillmore, 1850–1853
Franklin Pierce, 1853–1857
James Buchanan, 1857–1861
Abraham Lincoln, 1861–1865
Andrew Johnson, 1865–1869
Ulysses S. Grant, 1869–1877
Rutherford B. Hayes, 1877–1881
James A. Garfield, 1881
Chester Arthur, 1881–1885

Grover Cleveland, 1885–1889
Benjamin Harrison, 1889–1893
Grover Cleveland, 1893–1897
William McKinley, 1897–1901
Theodore Roosevelt, 1901–1909
William H. Taft, 1909–1913
Woodrow Wilson, 1913–1921
Warren G. Harding, 1921–1923
Calvin Coolidge, 1923–1929
Herbert Hoover, 1929–1933
Franklin D. Roosevelt, 1933–1945
Harry S. Truman, 1945–1953
Dwight D. Eisenhower, 1953–1961
John F. Kennedy, 1961–1963
Lyndon B. Johnson, 1963–1969
Richard M. Nixon, 1969–1974
Gerald R. Ford, 1974–1977
Jimmy Carter, 1977–1981
Ronald Reagan, 1981–1989
George H. W. Bush, 1989–1993
William J. Clinton, 1993–2001
George W. Bush, 2001–2009
Barack Obama, 2009–

Glossary

acceptance speech — a speech a politician gives when he or she wins an election

challenge — a difficult task

election — the act of choosing someone or deciding something by voting

equal rights — something that the law says a person can do; equal rights means a person is treated the same as someone else regardless of their race, age, or gender.

improve — to make better

popular — liked by many people

vote — to make a choice in an election

Read More

Grimes, Nikki. *Barack Obama: Son of Promise, Child of Hope*. New York: Simon & Schuster Books for Young Readers, 2008.

Nichols, Catherine. *Barack Obama*. Presidents of the U.S.A. Mankato, Minn.: Child's World, 2009.

Winter, Jonah. *Barack*. New York: Katherine Tegen Books, 2009.

Internet Sites

FactHound offers a safe, fun way to find Internet sites related to this book. All of the sites on Facthound have been researched by our staff.

Here's all you do:

Visit *www.facthound.com*

FactHound will fetch the best sites for you!

Index

basketball, 12

birth, 4

Chicago, Illinois, 12, 14, 22

Columbia University, 12

daughters, 18

election, 24

equal rights, 16

father, 4, 6

grandparents, 6, 10

Harvard University, 6, 14

Hawaii, 4, 6, 10

health care, 20

history, 24

Indonesia, 8

Iraq war, 20

jobs, 12, 20

mother, 4, 6, 8, 10

president, 18, 24, 26

Punahou School, 10

Robinson, Michelle, 14

senate, state, 16, 18

senate, U.S., 18

speeches, 20, 22

voting, 20, 22

Word Count: 353

Grade: 1

Early-Intervention Level: 24